This book belongs to:

__A Remarkable Person!__

'What Mental Disorder?' Book Series #3

Text Copyright © 2015 Jessie Shepherd

Illustrations Copyright © 2015 Tyler Shepherd

All rights reserved. This book or any portion thereof
may not be reproduced or used in any manner whatsoever
without the express written permission of the publisher
except for the use of brief quotations in a book review.

First Printing, 2015

ISBN 978-1-943880-12-6

Library of Congress Control Number 2015953720

Bluefox Press

Salt Lake City, UT 84121

Bluefoxpress.com

Vinny the Fox has PTSD

by jessie shepherd, ACMHC   illustrations ty shepherd

an imprint of
BlueFox Press

This is Vinny. He has Post Traumatic Stress Disorder. PTSD for short.

Vinny experienced an event in which he was in danger of death and injury.

NO LIFEGUARD ON DUTY

Lately, he has been having terrible nightmares.

Sometimes these nightmares are during the day and he can't tell what is real and what is not.

When he thinks back to the event, sections are missing. This makes him confused and frustrated.

Vinny gets startled easily. He is always paying attention to potential dangers around him.

Vinny is tough. But when he thinks about the event, he feels tiny and vulnerable.

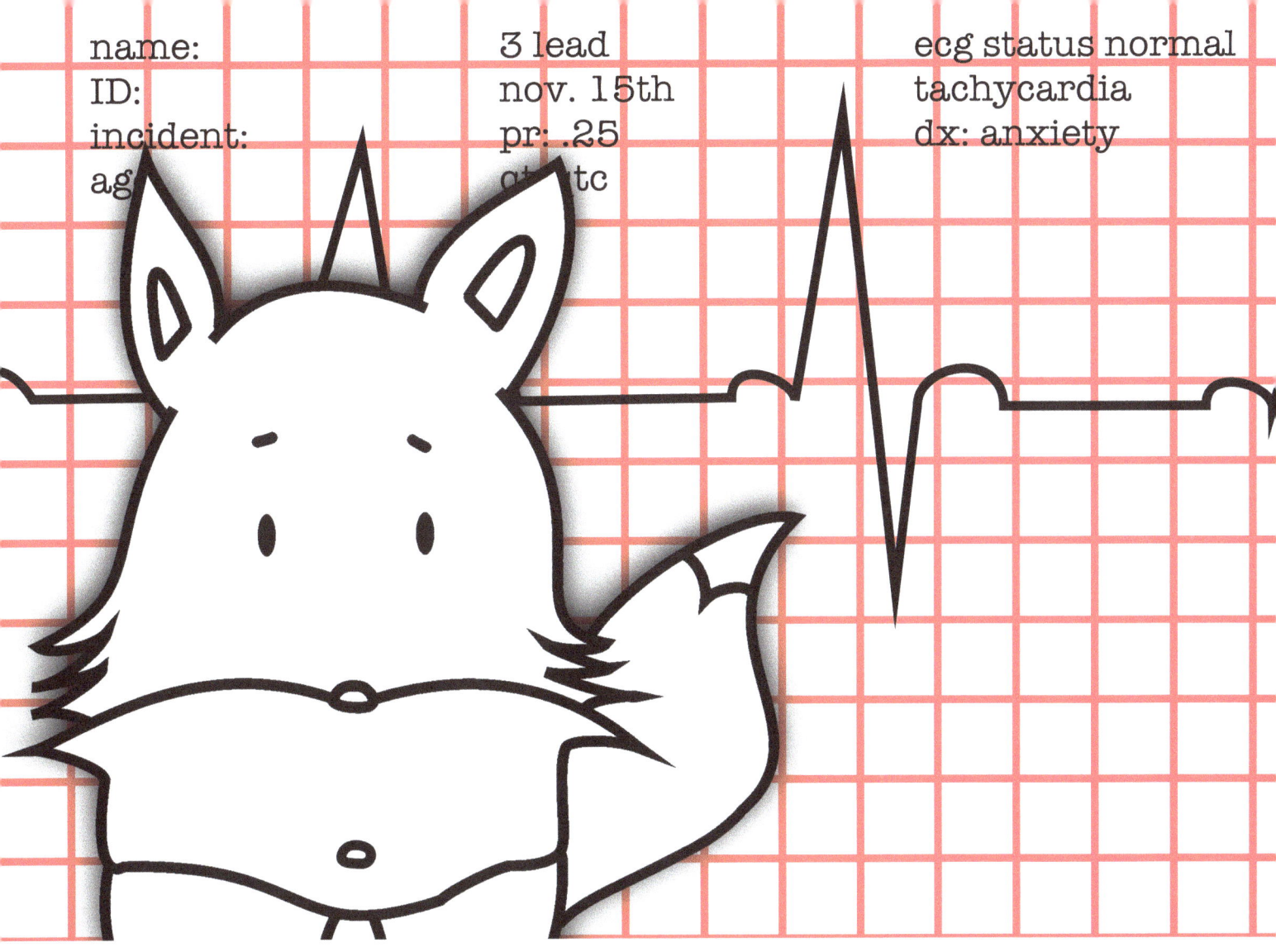

Sometimes his heart races. His stomach hurts. He gets sweaty. And he does not know why.

People think Vinny is irritable. He even has outbursts towards people he loves.

He doesn't want to push friends and family away.

He just feels detached.

He just feels numb.

He wants to hide away from anything social.

But Vinny can learn skills so he is not distressed anymore.

He can get help to process emotions about the event so he can enjoy life to the fullest.

Vinny can learn to take care of his needs so he feels safe and has a plan if overwhelmed.

Having Post Traumatic Stress Disorder has some inspiring parts too.

Like his strong sense of justice.

This fuels his fight for good to triumph.

He can easily see if someone is hurt or scared. Even when they are hiding it.

He wants to keep others safe so they don't experience what he did.

Vinny refuses to give up or be beaten.

Because of the event he can gain a better understanding of himself and his purpose.

Vinny is not alone and can find others that understand him.

Although he has suffered, he survived. This makes him incredibly strong.

Vinny is also courageous because he can rise from the ashes and prevail.

Best way to interact with someone with Post Traumatic Stress Disorder

- Understand that they are in a constant state of hyper-vigilance. This gets exhausting both mentally and physically.

- Have an exit strategy for events or situations that are upsetting to them such as fireworks, family reunions, holidays, crowds of people, etc. (Everyone is different)

- Create a plan with them on how to stay safe and cope with triggering situations.

- Seek professional support for you and your family. Eye Movement Desensitization Reprocessing (EMDR), Electroencephalographic Biofeedback (EEG - Neurofeedback), Congnitive Behavioral Therapy, along with forms of yoga have been shown to be effective treatment for PTSD. See a therapist for assessment and creating a personalized treatment plan.